TRACK & FIELD

Published by Creative Education, Inc.

123 South Broad Street, Mankato, MN 56001

Designed by Rita Marshall with the help of Thomas Lawton

Cover illustration by Rob Day, Lance Hidy Associates

Copyright © 1993 by Creative Education, Inc.

Photography by Allsport, Bettmann Archive, Duomo,
Focus on Sports, Sports Illustrated (James Drake, George
Tiedemann), Wide World Photos

Printed in the United States

Library of Congress Cataloging-in-Publication Data

Potts, Steve, 1956–

Track and Field / Steve Potts.

Summary: Presents "great" moments in Olympic history that
have taken place in track and field events, highlighting
performances by athletes that were particularly spectacular.

ISBN 0-88682-533-4

1. Track-athletics—History—Juvenile literature. 2. Track
and field athletes—United States—Biography—Juvenile
literature. 3. Olympics—History—Juvenile literature.
[1. Track and field—History. 2. Track and field athletes.
3. Olympics—History.] I. Title.

GV1060.5.P64   1992

796.42—dc20

92-3722

CIP

AC

TRACK & FIELD

S T E V E   P O T T S

CREATIVE EDUCATION INC.

High jumper Louise Ritter was not favored to win her event when she came to Seoul, South Korea, for the 1988 Olympics. The favorite was Stefka Kostadinova from Bulgaria. Kostadinova, the world-record holder at 6 feet, 10¼ inches, held a two-inch advantage over Ritter, whose best jump of 6 feet, 8 inches was an American record. Kostadinova was generally regarded as the first woman who had a chance to clear seven feet.

But Ritter was not about to give up.

Louise Ritter.

That morning in Seoul, September 30, 1988, both women easily cleared the bar during their early jumps. By the time the high jump bar reached 6 feet, 8 inches, all their competitors had dropped out. Kostadinova and Ritter, tied for first, had three tries at this height. Ritter missed all three. So did her rival. Kostadinova had the right height, but she came down hard on the bar. Officials announced a jump-off. Kostadinova and Ritter would get one more chance, and the first to clear the bar would win. If neither made the height of 6 feet, 8 inches, the bar would be lowered two centimeters at a time until either Kostadinova or Ritter cleared it. One would win the gold, one the silver, in their sport's greatest contest. Who would be number one?

Stefka Kostadinova.

AN OLYMPIC RECORD

For the heroes of track and field's great moments, success doesn't come without hard work. These athletes must spend long hours in training, always striving to improve their performances. They must be able to cope with the intense pressure of competition. And, sometimes, they must deal with the pain and frustration of being injured. But injuries have rarely stopped these committed athletes. Take, for instance, the case of determined Olympic sprinter Evelyn Ashford.

Sprinter Leroy Burrell positions himself in the starting blocks.

Born in 1957, Evelyn Ashford was one of five children. Her father was an Air Force sergeant. Being in the military meant moving often, and athletics gave Evelyn a way to meet new friends. But she wasn't always a star when it came to sports. When she was twelve, she decided to participate in the Junior Olympics. "The most important thing I remember about the Junior Olympics is that I came in dead last," Ashford admitted. "I was only twelve. I didn't know you had to be fit to compete."

Evelyn didn't give up, however. Her parents encouraged her to practice and to do her best. "I always had to be the one to set the example," she said. "If I did something wrong my mother would say, Look what you did, you have to set an example for your brothers and sisters. It wasn't always pleasant not to be able to do what you really wanted. But I think the reason I'm a good athlete is because I had to learn to do what I was told."

Evelyn Ashford.

All her hard work eventually won her one of the first women's athletic scholarships to UCLA in 1975. Her fast sprints won the attention of Pat Connally, UCLA's track coach and a three-time track and field Olympian. With Connally's encouragement, Ashford prepared for the 1976 Olympics. The training program was difficult, and there were many days of sore muscles, exhaustion, and tears. But the hard work paid off. The newcomer surprised Olympics fans by placing fifth in the 100-meter race at the Olympics in Montreal. It was the best finish by an American.

Rafer Johnson won the gold medal in the decathlon in the 1960 Olympics.

Hurdlers Roger Kingdom (left) and Tony Dees duel to the finish line.

During the next four years Evelyn Ashford prepared for the 1980 Moscow Olympics. Along the way she beat her top-ranked rival, East Germany's Marlies Gohr, at the 1979 World Cup meet in Montreal. Ashford's victory over the world-record holder was encouraging, but unfortunately, her hopes for the 1980 Olympics were dashed by politics. In protest of the Soviet invasion of Afghanistan, President Carter banned America's athletes from going to Moscow. Many other nations boycotted the Moscow Olympics as well.

Marlies Gohr (left) and Evelyn Ashford in close competition.

In May 1980, Ashford pulled a hamstring muscle at a Pepsi meet. Her injury put her out of competition for nearly a year. Dealing with her pain gave Ashford time to think. What did she want to accomplish? By 1981, her goal was clear. "I've given up a lot of things to be good at what I do. I want to win an Olympic medal," she asserted.

Preparing for the shot put.

Two years later, in 1983, Ashford set a 100-meter world record at the U.S. Olympic Festival in Colorado Springs. She seemed well on her way to achieving her goal. But another obstacle lay ahead. Only five weeks later, racing her rival Marlies Gohr at the World Championships in Helsinki, she tore another muscle. She dropped out of the race, her body in pain and her hopes for the 1984 Olympics in jeopardy.

Good competitors don't give up easily, however. Evelyn exercised her torn muscle and rebuilt her confidence. She tried not to worry and concentrated instead on doing her best. At the June 1984 Olympic Trials, she raced to victory in the 100-meter trials. Although twinges in her leg forced her to drop out of the 200-meter race, she had made the American Olympic squad. She was going to Los Angeles.

When Ashford lined up for the 100-meter race in Los Angeles on a warm summer day in 1984, she knew that America's hopes for the gold medal rested on her. She leaned over, put her feet against the starting blocks, and gazed ahead at the cinder track. The crowd shouted to their favorites and the stadium buzzed with talk,

Evelyn Ashford (third from left) jumps out of the starting blocks.

but the runners heard nothing. They concentrated on the race, knowing that a false start or a moment lost when the gun started could mean a lost race.

The gun sounded. The runners sprang forward out of the blocks, pulling themselves erect and pumping their legs. Ashford pushed ahead of the pack. As she strained across the finish line, her nearest rival was three feet behind. Ashford had won the race in 10.97 seconds—an Olympic record. The crowd rose, screaming her name and cheering wildly. American flags came out all over the stadium.

On the victory stand, Ashford wept tears of happiness as she waited to receive her gold medal. The enthusiasm of the crowd meant a great deal to her. "The response in the Olympic stadium today," she said, "tells me that I'm very much appreciated. Running fast and being good at what I do are reward enough for me right now."

Later during the 1984 Summer Games, Ashford added a second gold medal, this time in the 4 x 100 meter relay. After winning two gold medals and setting a world record, Evelyn Ashford could truly be called one of track and field's greats.

RUDOLPH'S TRIUMPH

Wilma Rudolph, one of Evelyn Ashford's childhood heroes, also ranks among track and field's greatest performers. She was the first American woman to win three gold medals in the Olympics, and her story is one of triumph over hardship.

Born in 1940 in Clarksville, Tennessee, Wilma Rudolph was the twentieth of twenty-two children. At the age of four, scarlet fever and double pneumonia struck Wilma, leaving her near death for several weeks. When she recovered, her left leg was paralyzed. The doctors were not hopeful. Yes, they told her mother, Wilma might recover, but she would need special treatment. For two years, Wilma's mother used her weekly day off to make the ninety-mile round trip to the clinic to get Wilma her treatments. The other six days Mrs. Rudolph came home from work, fixed supper for her large family, then sat down and massaged her daughter's leg. When Wilma failed to get better, three older children joined their mother's efforts and took turns massaging Wilma's paralyzed leg.

With her family's help, Wilma made remarkable progress. Soon she could walk a few steps, then even farther with a leg brace and special shoes. When her brother Westley bought a basketball, Wilma began playing with it—dribbling, shooting, and eventually even running. One day her mother came home and was amazed to find Wilma playing without her shoes. She no longer needed her brace. By the time she entered high school, she was even playing basketball on her school team. "Skeeter," as she was nicknamed by her high school basketball coach, eventually began running sprints. She won the girls' 50-, 75-, and 100-yard dashes in the state high school championships.

Carl Lewis won Olympic gold in the long jump in 1984 and 1988.

In the 1988 Olympics, Florence Griffith Joyner (left) captured first place in the 100- and 200-meter dashes.

Observing Rudolph's performance at the state track meet was Ed Stanley, coach of the Tennessee State University girls' track club, the "Tigerbelles." He offered her a work-study scholarship, allowing Rudolph, whose parents could not afford to send her to college, a chance at a higher education. By joining the team, Rudolph was able to work her way through Tennessee State.

The Tennessee Tigerbelles, with Wilma Rudolph at left.

The men's 100-meter finals at the 1991 World Championships in Tokyo.

Rudolph's hard work and constant practice paid off. Two months after her sixteenth birthday, in August 1956, she competed in the U.S. Olympic Trials. Her impressive times won her a place on the team, and she became one of the youngest competitors at the 1956 Olympics, held in Melbourne, Australia.

Rudolph's bronze medal in the 4 x 100 relay encouraged her, but Australian Betty Cuthbert's three gold medals convinced her to try for her own victories in 1960. She increased her training pace and her speed in college. Then, in November 1959, she came down with a painful sore throat. Her tonsils swelled, making breathing and eating nearly impossible. She was rushed to the hospital, where the doctor, after removing her infected tonsils, told her that they had probably weakened her for several years.

Wilma Rudolph (at left) breaks the tape in a semifinal heat in the 1960 Olympics.

Rudolph rebounded from her illness to complete her most successful season yet. Her greatest moment came in the 1960 Summer Olympics in Rome. Early on, bad luck plagued the young runner. Stepping in a hole during a practice, Rudolph twisted her ankle. Painfully she dragged herself to the grassy infield, lay down, and called for the team doctor. He gently turned her ankle, looked at the swelling, and told her she had sprained it. That night Rudolph packed her ankle in ice and rested. The next morning she cautiously stood up and tested her ankle. Taking a few steps, she stretched and carefully turned her leg. She could feel twinges of soreness, but it looked like she would be able to run.

Rudolph went on to win gold medals in the 100- and 200-meter races, breezing easily to victory and confounding those who thought that pain and a swelled ankle would keep her off the track. It was the 400-meter relay, however, that brought the Roman crowd to its feet. Rudolph anchored the American team, whose victory provided one of the most exciting moments of the 1960 Olympics.

Jackie Joyner-Kersee, winner of the 1988 Olympic heptathlon.

Wilma (at right) loses to fellow American Barbara Jones in a 1959 meet.

The Americans began the race as the favored team, and at first it looked like they would sail easily to another victory. After the starting pistol sounded, Rudolph's teammates Martha Hudson and Barbara Jones pumped the U.S. team into the lead. When the runners began the race's third leg, America's Lucinda Williams was leading.

On her handoff to Rudolph, however, Williams fumbled and staggered. The baton wobbled. Rudolph stopped, grabbed the baton from Williams, turned, and looked ahead. She was two full strides behind West Germany's Jutta Heine. Could she catch up? The crowd rose to its feet. With an incredible burst of power, Rudolph surged ahead. She had to make up for lost time. Just a few feet short of the finish line, she pushed past Heine and crossed the line barely ahead of her rival. The crowd of sixty thousand was in a frenzy. "Gazelle! Gazelle!" they shouted in a dozen languages. Rudolph responded to her nickname, turning to smile at her adoring fans. A stunned look was on her face. She was the first American woman to win three Olympic gold medals in track and field, a feat not matched until 1984.

In that final surge across the finish line in Rome, Wilma Rudolph provided the sport of track and field with one of its greatest moments.

17

Jackie Joyner-Kersee (center) in the 1984 Olympics.

Hurdler Greg Foster.

VAULTIN' BOB

The decathlon is one of the most challenging events in the Olympics. It is a combination of ten separate competitions that test an athlete's skill, speed, endurance, and strength. On the first day contestants participate in the 100- and 400-meter races, long jump, high jump, and shot put. The five events scheduled for the second day are the 110-meter hurdles, discus, javelin, pole vault, and, finally, the 1500-meter race. To win the Olympic decathlon is a great feat. To win two consecutive decathlons is one of track and field's most amazing accomplishments—and that's just what Bob Mathias did when he brought home gold medals from London (1948) and Helsinki (1952).

When Bob Mathias was in high school, his coach, Virgil Jackson, noticed his amazing ability as a hurdler and discus thrower and encouraged the sixteen-year-old to enter the decathlon. Mathias, who was also a standout in basketball and football, adapted easily to this new challenge. In 1948, at the age of seventeen, he won a place on the 1948 Olympic team after beating three-time U.S. champion Irv Mondschein.

Because of World War II, the Olympics had not been held since 1936. For many of the competitors who gathered in London for the 1948 Olympics, this meet represented the final chance to prove their abilities. In the decathlon, young Bob Mathias faced older and far more experienced men.

Decathlete Bob Mathias hurls the discus in the 1948 Olympics.

During the first day of competition Mathias held his own, but on the second day London's famous rain descended. The young Californian had never coped with bad weather. During the discus throw, rain and darkness made it nearly impossible to see the small metal pins and flags marking yardage. Although Mathias did well in all of his throws, a mishap prevented his best toss from being counted. Another contestant's throw knocked over Mathias's marker, and when decathlon officials went to measure the American's throw, they could not determine where the marker had

Bob Mathias repeats his success in the 1952 Helsinki Olympics.

been placed. Although they searched for almost an hour, they finally gave up and estimated its position. The officials' final ruling probably meant several lost feet. In an event where a slim margin can determine victory, those lost points were important.

The last three events—the pole vault, javelin, and 1500 meters—were lit only by flashlights. Because of the botched discus throw, they were vital to Mathias's victory. Mathias tried to remain confident. Cloaked in a rain-soaked blanket, he rested between events. Most of the crowd had already left; the rest tried to stay dry under blankets and tarpaulins.

In the end, everything rested on the 1500-meter race. Mathias was less than two hundred points behind France's Ignace Heinrich. To win the decathlon, the American would have to run the race in under six minutes.

In the darkness Mathias saw the starting gun's orange flash. He began running around the watery track, trying to forget about his stomach cramps and aching arms. He knew he had no chance of placing first in the 1500-meter race, but all he had to fight now was the clock. As he rounded the last stretch, Mathias gritted his teeth and began his sprint. He stag- gered across the finish line, plodded over to his parents in the stands, and waited for the official time. It was five minutes and eleven seconds! He had won!

The next day, better weather brought seventy thousand fans to the stadium. After officials gave Mathias his medal, the crowd began waving and cheering, and the band struck up "The Star-Spangled Ban- ner." Despite his excitement, Mathias still looked tired. "Never again, never again," he told his father after receiving the gold medal.

Carl Lewis (front), one of today's greatest track stars.

Mathias did return, however, and his performance in Helsinki in 1952 broke his own record as well as Galen Morris's 1936 Olympic record for American decathletes. This time the weather cooperated, but in his second try at the long jump Mathias pulled a muscle. Heat treatments and frequent rubdowns between events helped him through the remaining eight competitions. When he was done, he had compiled an astounding 7,887 points in ten events. Not until Rafer Johnson's amazing showing in the 1960 Olympics was Mathias's record broken.

In 1991, Mike Powell overtook Bob Beamon's twenty-three-year-old record in the long jump.

JENNER'S FINAL RACE

Spectators at the 1976 Olympics in Montreal witnessed an unforgettable performance by another great decathlete, Bruce Jenner. When he retired from competition

on July 30, 1976, Jenner looked back on a career that included a new world record, an Olympic title, and three straight years as the world's number-one-ranked decathlon champion. His American decathlon record stood for twelve years, a sign of his skill and ability as an athlete.

Daley Thompson, a decathlete from Great Britain.

Unlike Bob Mathias, who had trained little for the decathlon in 1948, Bruce Jenner devoted seven years of his life to preparing for his Olympic victory. His training program began at Graceland College in Lamoni, Iowa, where he was recruited to play football. There he caught the attention of L.D. Weldon, who had helped decathlete Jack Parker win a bronze medal at the 1936 Olympics in Berlin. Weldon convinced Jenner to try the decathlon. In Jenner's first meet, the Drake Relays in 1970, he took sixth place—and became hooked. He loved the decathlon.

Bruce Jenner throws the javelin in the 1976 Olympic trials.

Daley Thompson (left) won the Olympic decathlon in 1980 and 1984.

After a 1971 championship in the NAIA (National Association of Intercollegiate Athletics), Jenner finished tenth in the Munich Olympics in 1972. The next year brought him injuries, including a broken foot and an infected vertebra. But Jenner soon returned to form and in 1974 he claimed the first of three consecutive number-one world rankings.

Bruce Jenner competes in the pole vault.

Bruce Jenner's Olympic triumph in 1976 didn't come without a struggle. The lineup in Montreal included 1972 gold medalist Nikolay Avilov from the Soviet Union, as well as a powerful twenty-three-

year-old from West Germany, Guido Kratschmer. The competition was intense, and Jenner's victory wasn't assured until he took the lead after the eighth event, the pole vault. But while he was assured of a gold medal, what he really wanted was a world record.

East Germany's Christian Schenk won the Olympic decathlon in 1988.

Jenner's new record would depend on the last event, the 1500-meter run. When the gun sounded and the race began, the crowd was riveted to the track; many spectators had kept a running score and knew that Jenner was racing for a world record. As Jenner passed his wife Chrystie on the first lap, he heard her scream "Go, Bruce, please go!" His determination, his wife's encouragement, and the swell of noise from the stands pushed him onward. As he entered the last lap, Jenner knew he was going to win. "The more I picked up the pace, the better it felt," he said. "I couldn't have slowed down if I had wanted to. At the end I looked at the clock and saw I had the record. It was the happiest moment of my life."

A successful jump in the pole vault.

Thousands of people rose to their feet, waving flags and yelling. A young man rushed onto the track and handed Jenner an American flag. With the flag in hand, Jenner took his victory lap and joyfully met his wife at the finish line. At the awards ceremony he looked both tired and happy as he took the gold medal and kissed it. He deserved the title reserved for decathlon winners: "the world's greatest athlete."

Jenner's moment of victory.

Although Jenner retired from competition after the 1976 Olympics, he still maintains a deep interest in young athletes and their preparation for competition. "I've reached the level of my heroes, yet nothing has changed inside me," he said. "I'm the same guy I was when I was in junior high school. I haven't changed any."

Part of his success, Jenner feels, was his choice of the decathlon as his event. "Our society is based on specialists," he noted. "The decathlon goes against that. A decathlon is a presentation of moderation."

A GOLD MEDAL

The triumphs of Evelyn Ashford, Wilma Rudolph, Bob Mathias, and Bruce Jenner will always be counted among track and field's most exciting moments. Fans will remember, too, Louise Ritter's breathtaking final jump in Seoul.

Kastadinova was up first in the jump-off. She missed. Now everything rested on Ritter. This might be her last chance for a gold medal. She moved back for her take-off, paused a few seconds to assure herself that everything was right, took two walking steps and a small hop, and began running.

German Guido Kratschmer was one of Jenner's toughest competitors.

Eleven steps later Ritter angled at the bar from the right. She planted her left foot, sprang forward, and lofted over the bar. Now she was above it, only a breath from hitting it. As she fell her right thigh brushed against the bar, shaking it, but the bar stayed in place. She landed in the pit, lay there for a minute, then stood up. She had won a gold medal! Louise Ritter had demonstrated what training, concentration, and a winning attitude can do.

It was another great moment in track and field.

Louise Ritter captures the gold.